Best wishes

C. Denise Whitehead

21st CENTURY STEPFORD WIFE

The Modern Day Woman's Marriage and Relationship Survival Guide

C. DENISE WHITEHEAD, CPLC

authorHOUSE®

AuthorHouse™
1663 Liberty Drive
Bloomington, IN 47403
www.authorhouse.com
Phone: 1 (800) 839-8640

Published by AuthorHouse 10/03/2017

ISBN: 978-1-5462-0892-1 (sc)
ISBN: 978-1-5462-0890-7 (hc)
ISBN: 978-1-5462-0891-4 (e)

Library of Congress Control Number: 2017914822

Print information available on the last page.

This book is printed on acid-free paper.

CONTENTS

CONTENTS

There are instructions on how to put together everything, from electronics to furniture. Wouldn't it be great if marriage and relationships came with such a manual? What if you had instructions on how to troubleshoot or reboot a relationship drive? What if a manual told you what to do when a relationship freezes or stops working?

In 21st Century Stepford Wife, author Celia Whitehead presents a relationship/marriage survival guide. It offers insight into why some relationships survive while others fail. It teaches you to effectively communicate with your partner, and it discusses the information and tools necessary to navigate the complexities of relationships. Using an innovative analogy of the Stepford wives, the author revisits some of the traditional values that have been abandoned in the 21st century and applies them to modern-day relationships.

Touching on key principles to a happy and healthy relationship in each chapter, 21st Century Stepford Wife helps you simplify your relationship through tools, advice, and exercises gleaned from the author almost forty years of married life. This marriage know-how arsenal provides the keys to help couples avoid the pitfalls of divorce.

ACKNOWLEDGMENTS

I want to thank all the people who supported my dream to bring this book to the public. A special thank-you goes to my husband of thirty-nine years. Not only is he my inspiration; he is my biggest fan. When I doubted that I had a viable message to share, he assured me daily that this information would be of value. Thank you, Frank, for your input, as well as for your message to the men I hope will read this book with their wives and girlfriends.

I thank the couples who shared intimate stories about their relationship concerns and the difficulties they face in their marriages.

I give credit to Oprah Winfrey. I spent years as a loyal fan and watching all her makeover shows, which gave me the idea for a makeover for the 21st century woman.

I thank the mature women in my life who guided me with their pearls of wisdom, advice, and the occasional kick in the rear. In particular, I thank my grandmother for her love and guidance. I feel her presence with me daily, and her words of wisdom will forever remain in my heart.

If not for these women, I would not be the woman I am today.

Finally, I thank my daughter for sharing her life stories about dating and relationships in the 21st century. I am so proud of her, and I hope she finds a happy and healthy relationship.

CHAPTER 1

THE 21ST CENTURY STEPFORD WIFE

O kay. I can imagine what most of you are thinking right about now. Those of you familiar with *The Stepford Wives* movie, as well as the stereotype associated with it, must think I am pretty crazy. Those of you born after 1970 probably have no idea of what this reference means. Do not worry; I will give you more details in upcoming chapters.

Before I tell you what this book is about, let me tell you what it is not. It is not about women being subservient, weak, or doormats of any kind. I do not intend to set back the women's movement or imply that women do not deserve the same rights afforded to men. This book is meant not to criticize women's choices but to celebrate the fact that we do have choices in the 21st century. Marriage may appeal to some women but not to others. Those of us in relationships, whether married or cohabiting, all want happy and healthy bonding experiences. I celebrate all women, and I am grateful that we have the freedom to choose what works for our individual needs. This is not a one-size-fits-all diagram for relationships; it is a guide for women like me who have chosen one particular path.

Now let me tell you what this book is about.

It is about achieving a happy and healthy relationship by applying some of the traditional values that have somehow disappeared. Whether you are married, currently in a relationship, or hope to be in one someday, this book can help you maintain it and avoid some of the pitfalls most of us experience.

What do most women want? After speaking with numerous women, I've realized one common denominator is that we want happy and healthy relationships. The fundamental desire of most people, men and women, is to be happy.

Unfortunately, most of us are unsure about how to achieve that goal. At the beginning of a romance, we do not receive a manual with instructions on how to put a relationship together. I recently purchased a new Mac computer. I took it out of the box, plugged it in the wall, and quickly realized that I had no idea how to set it up. I pulled out the instructions and began reading. After spending a couple of hours downloading and upgrading software, I found myself working that computer like a pro.

There are instructions on how to put together everything, from electronics to furniture. Some instructions are easier to comprehend than others. I don't know about you, but when I read some manuals, I feel like I'm reading Greek instead of English. However, at least there are some guidelines to help you construct the product.

Wouldn't it be great if marriage and relationships came with such a manual? What if we had instructions on how to troubleshoot or reboot a relationship drive? What if a manual told us what to do when a relationship freezes or stops working?

It would reduce considerably the amount of stress and frustration we experience in our relationships. That is what I hope to accomplish for anyone reading this book. Let's start at the beginning.

From the day most women are born, we dream about finding the perfect mate, getting married, starting families, and living happily ever after. As little girls we dream about our wedding day, wearing a beautiful white dress and having all eyes upon us. In some cases, we spend an enormous amount of money on the big day. Our family members and friends are there to help us celebrate. We walk down the aisle toward the man with whom we intend to spend the rest of our lives. We recite our vows with anticipation and excitement.

After you are pronounced husband and wife, you celebrate with your family and friends. Afterward, you may even go on a fabulous honeymoon. When you return home, the guests are gone, the wedding gown is boxed up, and the rented tuxedo has been returned.

Reality sets in over time; differences of opinions, as well as major arguments, occur. You grow disenchanted because you now realize that relationships are not always like they are depicted in the movies. The reality of work, home, and day-to-day activities hits you like a ton of bricks. You suddenly realize that a relationship is not all hearts and flowers.

When difficult times arise, and they most certainly will, you probably will ask yourself, *What do I do now? How do I get through the difficult times in my relationship? How do I learn to communicate effectively? What can I do to prevent my marriage from becoming a divorce statistic?*

These are questions most of us in relationships will ask ourselves at some point. I asked myself these same questions at one point in my marriage. I had the same concerns that most women have in challenging times. I was lucky. Several matriarchs have helped guide and advise me over the years.

The advice and guidance I received, in addition to some of my own personal experiences, have allowed me to have a happy and healthy marriage for almost four decades. In this book, I will share with you the tools I have used over the years so that you too can enjoy success in your relationship. The last four decades have led me on a quest to understand relationships: why they work and why they don't. I started my search at my local bookstore. I read almost every book published on the subject, but I still needed more information. I knew there was no magic formula; however, there had to be some basic fundamentals to help me navigate the complexities of relationships. There had to be a common denominator among all the couples who had made it work. After all, it's not rocket science, as my grandmother used to say.

We get in our own way and make things more complicated than they have to be. This book will help you simplify your relationship, using the tools, advice, and exercises that helped me keep my relationship on the path to happiness and healthiness. I will share with you what I have learned so that, whether you are married today or hope to marry one day, you too can enjoy a happy and healthy relationship.

The Old Stepford Wife

Let's talk about the old Stepford wife and what she represented. Women, before you revoke my feminist card, and men, before you start celebrating, let me elaborate.

The Stepford wife was a character in a 1972 novel by Ira Levin called *The Stepford Wives*. In 1975, a movie based on the book was released in most major theater outlets. Several well-known actors of the time, including Katherine Ross and Peter Masterson, were cast in starring roles. The movie achieved marginal success at the box office; however, in recent years, it has developed a cult like following. Several remakes and sequels were made, including *Revenge of the Stepford Wives, The Stepford Children*, and a 2004 remake of the original. At the time the original movie was released, feminist groups did not approve and called it anti women and chauvinistic. A television ad advised wives to "see the movie before your husband does"; it was meant to serve as a warning for women. The cast responded to the criticism by saying that the movie was satirical, poked fun at traditional gender roles, and was not meant to be taken seriously.

What about the Stepford wife made so many women angry and excited so many men? Well, let's take a closer look at this character.

Both the movie and the book centered on a mythical Connecticut town. The women in this town were, well, perfect—perfectly manicured and made up, not a hair out of place. They looked pretty much like June Cleaver on the *Leave It to Beaver* TV show. You remember the look—lovely dresses, high heels, pearls, and red lipstick. These women cooked and cleaned all day with smiles on their faces. The wives treated their husbands like kings, making the men believe they were the best lovers women could have. The women's only goal was to take care of their homes and families. Wow, what a concept. Obviously, the husbands could not have been happier. Well, as it turned out, the actual wives had been replaced with robots.

You can see why neither book nor movie was viewed favorably by most women in the early 1970s.

You are probably thinking, *what in the world does women being duplicated as robots have to do with a happy and healthy relationship?*

The simple answer is—nothing at all. This book is about applying traditional values to modern-day relationships. It will not resonate with every woman, and it is not meant to. This book is for women like me who made the conscious decision to make our husbands, homes, and families our number one priority. It is meant not to criticize those who made different decisions but rather to support those who have chosen this path.

The 21st Century Stepford Wife

Who or what is a 21st century Stepford wife? She is a woman who is educated, smart, worldly, funny, and attractive; above all, she loves her family. Her home and family are her top priority. She may or may not have had a career outside of the home. First and foremost, she is a woman who unashamedly loves and respects her husband. *She is me.*

My story begins one Christmas holiday when a male friend was visiting. We began a discussion about modern-day relationships. He'd been divorced three times. He told me some stories about his dating history, as well as his failed marriages. I'd known this individual for the better part of twenty years, so I had a pretty good idea of what went wrong. But I asked him why he thought his marriages had failed.

After a few minutes of contemplation, he began to ramble on about how his wives would not listen to him, were too opinionated, and were more concerned with material things that other women had. I knew this man was opinionated and controlling of women, and I suspected that was why his marriages failed. He liked to control how his wife dressed, how she wore her hair, and the image she presented in public.

I asked him what he wanted in a relationship and in a woman in particular. After a few moments of thought, he gave an answer that was not at all surprising and confirmed that my original assessment of his failed relationships was correct. He said he wanted a woman who worshipped him, whose sole existence was to make him happy. I just about choked on the peanuts I was eating, shocked at his honesty. I'm sure many men share his sentiment, but how many have the courage or stupidity to be so honest?

I needed a few minutes to absorb his answer before I could give an intelligent response that did not include kicking him out of my house. After collecting my thoughts, I told him, "You don't want a wife. You want a robot. You want a Stepford wife."

Much to my surprise again, he responded, "That's exactly what I want."

Now totally mortified, I asked, "Is that really what you want? A woman with no brain, no thoughts of her own, just someone to take care of you!"

After a few moments of silence, he said, "Well, when you put it that way, it does sound pretty chauvinistic."

"You think so?" I replied. We both sat in silence for a few minutes trying to digest the conversation.

Finally he said, "You know what I want? A woman like you. You are a modern-day Stepford wife."

Let me tell you—I just about exploded. I could not believe he'd called me a Stepford wife. *Did he just call me a robot?* I thought to myself. *Was he implying that I was a mindless android unit? Oh no he didn't!* I prepared my mind to do verbal battle with him for that insult he'd just hurled at me.

He sensed that I was becoming irate; the fact that I was turning beet red must have given it away. "Before you get upset, let me clarify my position," he said.

Yes, you do that, I thought to myself. *How dare this man insult me in my own home?*

"I watch the way you take care of your husband," he said. "You keep the house clean, cook, buy his clothes, and anticipate his needs. You know what he wants and needs before he utters a word. You make sure he takes his medicine and goes to his doctor's appointments each year.

"He doesn't even know his social security number and has to ask you for it. When you are helping out with the business, you make sure he has all the conveniences he needs to make his day more comfortable. It reminds me of how my grandmother took care of my granddad. You just don't see women caring for their men like that today. That is what I miss; that is what I really want.

"So many modern-day women have the 'I don't need a man' attitude, and they don't seem to want to put much energy into relationships. Today's women are career driven and materialistic. They are more concerned with the size of the diamond ring you put on their fingers and the size of their houses."

Okay, he redeemed himself, and I had to admit he did make a good argument. Again, we sat in silence for a few minutes.

"So, the type of woman I want—who does she sound like?" he asked.

Well, when he put it like that, I guess I did sound a little like a Stepford wife. It took a few days for me to digest the entire conversation. I must admit the new revelation did not sit well with me. I put the conversation out of my mind for the rest of the holiday season. As spring approached, I decided to revisit the conversation that had remained stuck in the back of my mind. *Stepford wife. Really? Me?* I had a successful career. I held high-level management positions with company cars (Mercedes Benz, mind you). I traveled for business on Lear jets. I even met Vice President Dan Quayle at a business conference in Washington, DC.

I have always thought of myself as a progressive woman. I am intelligent, well traveled, and well respected. However, while I did enjoy the accolades of being a career woman and making a lot of money, I must admit I have never been happier than I am today. Yes, I do keep my house clean—no housekeeper—and, yes, I unashamedly love and take care of my husband. But does that make me a Stepford wife?

After a few more weeks of contemplation—as you can see, I struggled with this—I thought to myself, *so what if I am a Stepford wife?* I mean, minus the whole robot thing, what did she do that was so wrong? She took care of her family. Okay, I do that. What else? She respected her husband as the head of the household. What's wrong with that?

She praised her husband, cooked for him, and made him feel like the gifted lover he was. The more I thought about it, the less offended I was about the comparison. At that moment I had what Oprah calls an aha moment; clarity washed over me. What the Stepford wife needed was a modern-day makeover.

I'd spent many years watching Oprah give makeovers to deserving viewers, and I decided to take a page from her book. After all, nobody does makeovers better than the incomparable Miss O.

I decided to give the old version of the Stepford wife a twenty-first-century makeover. And so it began. She is no longer a robot who cooks and cleans in stilettos and pearls all day. She definitely does not wander around the house waiting for her husband to come home. She is a 21st century woman who embodies some of the traditional values of the 1950s that we've somehow lost in this century.

She enjoys taking care of her family and home but does so out of love and respect, not obligation. This is a woman who is intelligent and worldly with opinions of her own. She made the choice to make her family and relationship her number one priority.

I guess I am a Stepford wife, a 21st century Stepford wife, and proud of it.

Let me tell you, I wasn't always this person. Like many women, I worked and had a successful career. I made a lot of money and traveled extensively. During the early years of my marriage, I was relatively happy. Both of us worked, paid bills, and spent a minimal amount of time together. It seemed like we had it together. That is until one day, it hit me. I felt like a zombie, each day doing the same thing as the day before.

Boredom set in, like it does for most people who have been married more than a decade. I wondered, *is this all there is to life and marriage?* I felt more like my husband's roommate than his wife. Yes, we did take the occasional vacation and tried to spend as much time together as our schedules allowed, but it never seemed enough. We continued this same routine for another decade until that fateful day when we both looked at each other and almost simultaneously admitted that we were not satisfied with our relationship.

Faced with the dilemma that most couples encounter at some point, we knew we had to make some changes if the relationship were to survive. I began to research marriage and relationships. I was a constant fixture at Borders and Barnes and Noble bookstores. I read almost everything I could find on the subject. I attended a few relationship workshops. I knew I loved my husband, and I wanted to keep my marriage together, so I was determined to find the formula to make that happen. In business, I was relentless and successful, and I wanted to apply those principles to my relationship as well.

What I learned after weeks of reading and talking to other couples was that relationships are ever-changing and evolving. I realized that to sustain a relationship, both people have to evolve and grow together. Relationships are not romance novels.

Wouldn't it be great if our husbands were like the handsome men in the romance novels, telling us how beautiful we are and bringing us flowers and making passionate love to us every day? Well, I don't know about you, but I think that would be boring after the first few decades. I guess that would not be terribly realistic. You rarely get a realistic view of relationships from books and the movies.

My first step was to throw out the movie version of a relationship and make my own determination. I approached the situation from a business perspective. I asked my husband to join me on a weekend retreat. When we arrived at our destination, I asked him to write a brief novel outlining what he wanted our marriage to be. He was confused at first, but I thought it would be a good exercise to see if we were on the same page and wanted the same things.

I did the same. Boy, did we have many rewrites. On Sunday afternoon, we went to brunch. *Reading each other's novels may be easier to digest after a good meal and a few mimosas*, I thought. It turns out I was right. We were both so nervous about the thought of bearing our souls. You would think that after so many years of marriage, we would know all there was to know about each other. Boy, were we wrong. After reading each other's papers, we sat in silence for a few minutes.

Then, the most amazing thing happened. We both began to laugh hysterically.

You see, we had each written quite the same thing. I'd always thought my husband wanted a modern-day career woman, someone who worked and bought home the bacon. It was 1998, and I fancied myself to be a twentieth-century modern woman. Yes, I was a wife and mother, but I could also close a business deal with the best of the good old boys. I was a twentieth-century woman.

Well, it turns out my husband wanted just the opposite. And, according to my novel, so did I. As much as I enjoyed wearing my modern-day woman hat, I actually longed to be a modern-day housewife. Sounds crazy, right? What I wanted more than anything else was to be a better mother and wife. While my career flourished at the time, my job as wife and mother was not quite as successful. I wanted to be successful in those areas as well, but I knew that meant I had to make some difficult choices.

I had to decide what was more important—traveling and making money or having a happy and healthy relationship. I chose the latter, a decision that started me on the path to where I am today.

Don't misunderstand; while I finally have the happiness I sought after, it isn't hearts and flowers every day. What I have learned is how to navigate marriage so that the hearts and flowers days come more often than not. I have learned to work through the challenging days that surely come in every relationship.

Each and every day is a new opportunity to create the relationship that you desire. In the upcoming chapters I will share with you the techniques that I learned over the last two and a half decades that allowed me to arrive at this place.

Before we get to the marriage section, let's start at the beginning. Before marriage comes the dating ritual. How you date and what you learn during this crucial period will determine the course of the marriage, particularly in this new era of social media and online dating.

CHAPTER 2

DATING IN THE INFORMATION AND SOCIAL MEDIA AGE

Dating is a lot like trying to find a parking space. The good ones are taken, and the rest are handicapped.

T hese days, many single people probably agree with that comment.

Although this book is about achieving a successful and healthy marriage, I believe it is important to begin with how we get there. How we date determines the course of the relationship.

Dating rituals have changed dramatically over the last decade. Given Facebook, Instagram, and the numerous online dating sites that exist, it's a wonder anyone can keep up. Technology has become a double-edged sword. While it has made our lives more convenient, it has taken away our ability to communicate verbally. Is it any wonder that when difficulties arise we don't know how to talk to each other?

I watched my daughter carry on a conversation with a male friend one day; the entire conversation took place via text. She would send a text and wait for a response. After reading his response, she would text again. After watching this for about an hour, I asked why she didn't just call her friend and have a civilized conversation. She informed me that young people today don't call unless they have to; anyway, texting was faster and easier. Is it any wonder that couples today have a difficult time talking to each other? If people do not have effective communication skills, their relationships are doomed to fail. You can't text or e-mail your way out of an argument. Again, your dating experiences will show you how the marriage will unfold.

In today's society, people believe it is acceptable to text, rather than call, and invite someone out with a few minutes' notice. There is little to no preparation involved in dating these days. Much has changed since I was a young girl. Back in my day—that sounds so out of touch—a young man called you on a landline; we didn't have cell phones back then. If the young man didn't call by Wednesday for a weekend date, the young lady wouldn't accept, as that wasn't considered proper. Attitudes toward dating and relationships have changed dramatically in the 21st century.

We have evolved into a hookup generation, for whom sex on the first date is not only acceptable but expected. When did the tide turn? I wanted more insight, so I decided to go directly to the source: young people.

I interviewed ten young women between the ages of sixteen and thirty-two. All were single; some were in relationships, and others were dating without commitment. What I found was eye-opening. I asked all ten young ladies how many had had sexual relations. All but one said she had, even the sixteen-year-old. Five out of the ten admitted to having had sex on the first date, again, including the youngest member of the group. I asked if they did so because they'd felt pressure from the guy. Only one indicated that she'd felt if she didn't comply, the guy would not call her again. The others said that they had wanted to and thought it was okay to do so. I was surprised by their candor. *Why has this behavior become the norm*, I asked myself? I asked the twenty-two-year old, who had said she was still a virgin, what influenced her decision to refrain from having sex? From an early age, she told me, both of her parents had instilled in her a strong respect for her body, and she demanded the same from her male counterparts. She was not saving herself until marriage, but rather she had not met a man with whom she felt enough of a connection with to share that special part of herself. I had to applaud her conviction and her parental influence. However, I felt no closer to understanding this phenomenon of acceptance of casual sexual encounters.

I wonder if the wide gap between the ratio of women to men has caused some women to feel that their options are limited; therefore, they give in more quickly and easily. Music videos depict women as little more than sex objects to be passed around. Is it any wonder that some young women find it acceptable to have sex without even knowing the guy's last name.

Now I am not suggesting that we return to the 1950s style of dating, as I know some young people deem it old-fashioned, but we need to restore the respect we seem to have lost in the 21st century. If we are to have successful relationships and marriages, we must lay the foundation at the beginning, during the dating process. Young men must be willing to trust and respect women, and women must demand their respect. It may mean your dating pool will be reduced, but in the end, it's about the longevity of the relationship, not a single date.

If you want to be a wife, you must think and act like a wife. Carry yourself and dress in a manner that when a man see's you in public the first thought that comes to his mind is, she is wife material and not just someone I want to take home for a night. You want to be the girl that he calls for a date or even better, several dates.Setting high standards can be the difference between him taking you to meet his family or him taking you to the waffle house the morning after. Moral and standards are not old fashioned nor out of date.

I am often asked by single women, why do I keep attracting the same type of man?

What you attract is based on the energy you put out into the Universe. If you send out energy that suggest it may be easy to get you into bed, you will continue to attract men who are only interested in one night stands. It can be something as simple as your body language or the way you dress. Sorry ladies, but if you dress provocatively and leave little to the imagination there will be one thought on his mind and it won't be boy she would make a good wife and mother.

In addition, you don't want to come off as being desperate for a husband either. That will make a man run away faster than if he were running out of a burning building. A secure woman is an attractive woman. Keep calm and carry on as the slogan suggest. This certainly applies to dating in the 21st century.

Here is a piece of advice about men for young women dating today. Men are not on the same timetable as women when it comes to marriage. A man will tell you that as long as the relationship is working, there is no reason to add a piece of paper to it. Remember the wedding day is primarily for the woman and her family and friends. For most men, their primary responsibilities are to secure the tux, pay for the wedding, and show up at the church on time. They say "I do," celebrate, and go on the honeymoon. Job done.

In their minds, nothing will change for them, so why go through all the hoopla and spend a small fortune on one day. Men don't dream about the day they will walk down the aisle on their wedding day, beautifully dressed, and with all eyes on them. Due to biological clocks and societal pressures, women tend to feel more of an urge to marry than men do. Biological clocks are not the same for men as they are for women. As a result, some women will pressure a guy to pop the question before he is ready to do so.

As Steve Harvey tells women all the time, no amount of pressure or ultimatums will make him marry you. He has to come to that decision on his own. Now, that's not to suggest that a woman should wait an indefinite amount of time before he drops to one knee and pops the question. Only you can decide what that timeline is. Just remember you cannot and should not force marriage; those who do usually end up divorced.

I am going to share some tips with you single ladies to get you closer to the brass, or rather, the platinum and diamond ring.

In order to get that guy that you are so crazy about to commit, you must think like the 21st century Stepford wife. She understands him, and she makes herself indispensable to him.

A man will commit to you—*listen to this, ladies, it is important*—at the point he knows his life is better and more fulfilling with you in it. Until he comes to that realization, he will not commit. That's why I feel that this marriage model can work. If you apply the tools in this book, you may find yourself picking out that dress and planning that big day a lot sooner than you'd planned.

I have spoken with several single men of all ages and races, and I have watched enough shows about dating and relationships to know that men view commitment differently than women. Have you ever read *Men are from Mars and Women are from Venus*? While I am not endorsing this book, I do agree with the fundamentals. Men and women are wired differently. Single men want women who make them feel like kings. Trust me, ladies—if you treat him like a king, he will willingly make you his queen.

That may sound sexist to some of you, but it is the truth.

Let me share a story about a young man in his late thirties; he was successful, good looking, and educated. He dated several women of all races and ages, yet he was not willing to commit to any one woman. Initially, I thought he was a player who liked dating several women at a time. After getting to know him better and several conversations later, I realized that while he did enjoy dating, he wanted nothing more than to settle down with a partner to whom he could relate. He was looking for someone who made him feel respected and above all needed—and not just for his bank account.

A man needs to feel like he is the king of the castle. Women tend to make most of the household decisions, but the man of the house needs to feel not only like the provider and protector but also like the leader of the family. Men want a cheerleader, who is always there to encourage them, especially during difficult times.

I have always said that a woman should be her man's biggest cheerleader.

I was listening to the radio and a song called "Cheerleader" came on the air. As I listened to the words, I thought to myself, *Who is this man? Is he reading my mind?* He was singing about the woman in his life, and he called her his cheerleader. He sang about how other women wanted to make him cheat, but he refused because his woman was always there for him, gave him love and affection, and was his biggest cheerleader. He sang about how she motivated him and gave him love when he needed it. His mother liked her and the only thing left for him to do was to pop the question. Bingo.

Wow, I thought to myself. *Here I am listening to a man sing the exact same thing I had been saying for years.* I felt total validation, knowing that I was on to something. Men want a woman who will not judge them but respect them and cheer them on. Just as in sports, the cheerleaders chant the cheers and lift the team up even when they are losing. This is what our men want and need.

Another favorite quote of mine is, "Just like in a game of chess, the queen protects the king." Let him know that you trust him to lead and that you have his back.

I came across a picture on the Internet of a woman leaning against her husband's back with him facing forward. The caption above the woman read, "I stand behind you because I trust you to lead the way"; above his head, the caption read, "I lead the way, because I know you always have my back." This is the true essence of what a relationship should be—him, leading the way, and you having his back. That is what most men are looking for.

There is one other point I would like to make. I know it's a touchy subject, but I hear this from men constantly: don't ask a man to buy you a new bag or a new pair of shoes on the first or second date. Most men are not interested in your bills or your money troubles early in the relationship. They indicate that this is a big turnoff. It makes them feel as though you are only dating them for financial gain. This is the basis for the term *gold digger*. A man, especially if wealthy, doesn't want to feel that you are only interested in his wallet. Show interest in him, not in what he can do for you. As the relationship progresses, most men will want to make you happy and to please you. The gifts will come if the relationship endures; however, you never want to make him feel like an ATM.

Lastly, and probably most importantly do not bring the baggage from your previous relationship into the next one. Anyone who has ever dated has a story of loss, disappointment or betrayal. You can't make the new man in your life pay for the sins of the last man. Clean the slate and unpack the baggage from that old trunk of hurt and sadness. Start fresh and don't assume that every man is the same as the last one. He can't and will not pay for another's transgressions. Let go of previous loss and start anew.

Remember, ladies, you want to entice and encourage, not badger and blackmail, your man into marrying you. Try applying some of these tips; what do you have to lose? You must have standards to which a man must adhere. Require him to show respect for you. Always act and expect to be treated like a lady. What you require is what you will receive. Follow these tips, and that platinum ring and white dress may be just around the corner.

Go out, date, and have fun. See where it takes you.

CHAPTER 3

MARRIAGE: HOW TO ACHIEVE A SUCCESSFUL RELATIONSHIP

Neither the size of your diamond nor the extravagance

of your wedding will make your marriage last.

That takes something money cannot buy.

Merriam-Webster's Dictionary defines marriage as "the state of being united to a person in a consensual and contractual relationship recognized by law." Common-law marriage is defined as being in a consensual state of marriage without a legal contract. Most states within the union recognize common-law marriage as a legal contract, usually after a period of cohabitation. Whether you are in a contractual or a common-law marriage, however, the challenges are the same.

First, let me say that there is no magic formula for a happy marriage. No matter their race, religion, politics, ethnicity, or social background, most women want the same thing—for our families and relationships to be happy and healthy. As mentioned previously, I don't suggest that the methods I discuss in this book will appeal or apply to every woman. There is more than one road map to happiness. Only you, as a woman, can decide which route to take. What I will share with you is what I have learned during the course of my marriage, and I am still learning about what works. I believe it is important to continually grow and learn about one's relationship. When you stop learning about each other boredom sets in. Even today, I am amazed when I learn something new about my husband. Just when I thought I knew everything about him, I learn something new. I find that fascinating.

Marriage in the 21st Century

Marriage and relationships are vastly different today than they were in our parents' and grandparents' eras. In the past, roles were more gender specific. A woman usually stayed home and took care of the house and children while the man went to work and provided financially for the family. She cooked, cleaned, and tended to the needs of the family. He was considered the head of the household and made most of the decisions. For most women, finding a husband and getting married was a top priority. Before the 1960s, there weren't many career opportunities for women. Marriage, therefore, was viewed by many women as their only means for financial security.

This, however, has changed over the last fifty years. Women today have many more career opportunities than women in previous generations did. We are now captains of industry and media moguls and run major corporations. Marriage is no longer our only opportunity for financial security.

Today, we certainly are enjoying the fruits of the women's liberation movement, which afforded us many opportunities. It has not been without consequences though. The divorce rate is higher than it's ever been in recorded history. More women head single-family households than ever before.

According to Bloomberg News, single Americans make up

more than half of the adult population for the first time since the government began compiling these statistics in 1976. I found this information quite disturbing. What happened? What can be done? How can we extend our relationships so that they don't become another statistic?

While every relationship is unique and different, there are some basic fundamentals that can extend the life of a relationship. The top five that immediately come to my mind are as follows:

1. Respect
2. Communication
3. Trust
4. Loyalty
5. Love

Women all have similar goals for our relationships and families. We want happy and healthy relationships. We want our children to be happy and healthy, and we want our men to love us (okay, and treat us like queens). How do we get there?

I will share with you how I got there and achieved a relationship that is happy, healthy, and enduring.

At the time I wrote this book, I had been married thirty-nine years. I married at the tender age of eighteen, and my husband was twenty-two.

I grew up in the Midwest in a large family and was raised by my paternal grandmother. She raised nine children on her own, including my younger brother and me, after her husband passed away. She did so without complaint or concern about her own needs or happiness. I watched her work long hours and then return home and cook some of the best meals you can imagine. She often went without a new coat or new shoes so her children would have what they needed.

At her knee, I gained valuable insight into relationships. She taught me the value of relationships and taking care of the family. Most important, she taught me how to take care of a man and remain a strong and capable woman. She also taught me how to make an awesome sweet potato pie.

My grandmother was not happy that I married so young, but she eventually came around. From her, I learned so much about what it means to be a woman. She taught me how to value myself and never settle for less than I deserved—a trait I apply to this day. She told me about her parents, the love they shared despite extreme challenges, and how they weathered the storms they faced. I loved hearing her stories. Marriage in her day, as she put it, was forever. There were no seventy-two-day marriages. Unless there was abuse in some form, you stayed in the marriage. Period.

Today, marriages and relationships have become disposable

and interchangeable. If it doesn't work out, find another. I am not sure what made the tide change, and when that occurred, but it most certainly was not the best thing that happened to families.

Another matriarch guided me in the early years of marriage— my mother-in-law. Admittedly, we did not always have the best relationship, but she did pass on some pearls of wisdom. Let me share one story with you; I still apply its lessons in my daily life. One Sunday after church, we were eating dinner at my mother-in-law's home. I had been married less than a year at the time. My husband worked that day and was pretty tired by the time he reached her house. He asked me to fix him a plate of food. I responded by asking, "Is there something wrong with your feet and hands?"

My mother-in-law took me aside and told me that when a man works all day, it is his wife's duty, at the very least, to fix his plate. I apologized to my husband and promptly fixed him a big plate of food. To this very day I still prepare plate of food for him when he comes home from work. Every day he tells me how much that little gesture means to him.

My grandmother's advice and wisdom helped us get through some difficult times early in our marriage. One night my husband and I had a really big fight. To this day, I do not remember what the fight was about. I got on my high horse and decided I was leaving him. I packed up our one-year-old daughter, and off to Grandma's house I went.

She let me vent and carry on for a while. Of course, it was entirely his fault. I took no blame at all. She listened, as she always did. I told her I wanted to divorce him and move back home. She calmly fixed me a plate of food and told me to put the baby down for a nap. After we ate, she looked me in the eye and asked if I had gotten all the drama off my chest. I was a bit confused by her question.

She asked if I'd been hurt physically during the argument. I responded, "Of course not."

She asked me if I'd thought I was in any kind of danger. Again, I answered, "Of course not."

"Are you fearful to be in your home?" she asked

"No," I answered. "Where is this going?"

She told me that if I did not fear for my life or safety, then it was time for me to go home and work things out with my husband. You don't run out on your marriage because you have an argument or disagreement, she said. To add insult to injury, she had me fix him a plate of food since I had not been home to cook. As you can see, much of my life revolves around plates of food.

As angry as I was at the time, I now know she was completely right. She reminded me about the vows I'd recited on our wedding day. You know, the ones about for better or worse, richer or poorer, sickness and in health, and in good times and bad. Okay, I had agreed with those vows. She had a point.

I swallowed my pride and went home. To this day I cite that as the best advice I could have been given at the time. Had she given me any other advice, I might not be with my husband today. (Thanks, Gran.) Over the years, she imparted home-grown wisdom that I took to heart and share with other couples experiencing difficult periods in their relationships.

This chapter features tips and tools that I use to maintain harmony in my marriage. These tools can be helpful whether you are married or in a relationship and hope to be married one day. This information is designed to help like-minded women. It is not intended as a criticism for women who have chosen a different path. Let me say that again. I am not criticizing any woman for making her choices. My goal is to share information with my sister-women.

As a life coach who specializes in relationships. I frequently host couples workshops in my home. During these workshops, we discuss difficulties faced by each couple and ways they can overcome them. I share the same information with my clients that I am sharing with you. (The couples often tell me to put this information in a book, and here we are. After much debate and a hundred reasons I gave to myself for not giving in, I finally decided to put what I know in a manual in the hope that someone would benefit.) Let's start with the basics.

Over the years, I have found a few basic fundamentals that will help you to build a solid foundation for your relationship. In addition, I will share quotes from various sources that were sources of comfort to me during challenging times.

The first law of marriage is no two days will be the same. There will be good days and bad days. There will be romance as well as dry spells. You may have financial difficulties. At some point in time, one or both of you may experience health challenges. The good news is you get to go through it together. Two is always better than one. I don't know about you, but I would much rather go through illness, financial difficulties, and family problems with the person I love and chose to share my life with than face those challenges alone.

Marriage Is a Job

Marriage is like a job at a post office, bank, or real estate company. To be successful and remain employed, you will have to meet your employer's expectations. Sometimes there is an employment contract. Your marriage contract comprises the wedding vows you recited. You agreed to certain conditions just as you would if you worked for the post office.

If you don't show up to work on time and perform the task for which you are paid, what happens? I'll tell you what happens: you will be terminated. Usually the first step is a verbal warning, which is followed by a written warning, probation, and eventually termination.

The same thing happens in a relationship; only it's called divorce. Rarely does anyone wake up one day and decide that she wants a divorce. There were warning signs along the way, but they were either ignored or avoided. To avoid termination or divorce, you have to show up every day and do the work.

The work does not have to boring or mundane. You get out of it what you put in it. Understanding this concept will take you further than most couples ever get.

No Two Years Will Be the Same

There will be good years, bad years, and just getting by years. And that's okay; every day will not be hearts and flowers. But that makes the good days and good years so much better. A marriage certificate does not guarantee you will be together forever; it's only paper. It takes love, respect, trust, understanding, friendship, and faith in your relationship to make it last. Love will not always be magic and fireworks. Sometimes it's felt in patience and acceptance.

I was watching a movie about an elderly couple who had been together for several decades. A young man asked the wife how many years she'd been happily married. The woman answered, "Twenty-seven years."

The husband looked at her like Alzheimer's was setting in. Then he said, lovingly, "Sweetie, we have been married forty-five years."

She laughed and said, "I know that. He asked how many years I had been happily married, and I told him the truth—twenty-seven years." She told the young man that not every year of a marriage is bliss. Some years will be difficult; that is inevitable. If you build a solid foundation you will be able to withstand those years and the difficult times, she said.

A famous comedian talked about marriage during one of his standup shows. He said that a couple had not been married long enough until one of them had contemplated murder and was stopped only by the episode of *CSI* where the husband killed his wife and was caught. Some of us can identify with his sentiment. Sadly, the comedian and his wife filed for divorce, still a much better option than murder.

I am thirty-nine years into my marriage, and if I were to

count, I would have to say there have been thirty-three good years, which is not too bad, I think. During some of those years, I might have had thoughts of murder floating around in my head. The *CSI* episode did not stop me. Instead, I remembered why I got married in the first place and hung in there until the difficult period passed. And pass it did. As my grandmother used to say, "The storms will come, but if you have a strong enough ship, you will make it to shore with the sun on your face and the wind at your back."

Friendship

The elderly woman in the movie explained that she and her husband had a friendship above all else. No matter what happened, that friendship sustained them. I could not agree more with this wise woman. My husband and I are best friends. While we both have outside friendships, none can compare to the one we share. I saw an anonymous post on the Internet that read, "It's not a lack of love, but rather a lack of friendship that makes unhappy marriages." Again, I could not agree more.

Be One Another's Top Priority

Granted, we all have interests outside the home—work, friends, outside hobbies and activities. But we must not lose track of one another.

Remember—this is part of the job. "Good relationships don't just happen. They take time, patience, and two people who truly want to be together and are willing to do the work." I hear all the time that a good marriage is one where each person contributes 50 percent. I say hogwash!

A strong marriage rarely has two strong people at the same time. Sometimes a husband and wife must take turns being strong for each other during the moments when the other feels weak. There will be times when you may be capable of giving only 20 percent, and he has to make up the remaining 80 percent. Some days it will be in reverse; you may have to give 70 percent while he gives 30 percent. It takes whatever it takes to make the relationship work.

The percentage given by each person will change from time to time. And that's okay as long as one person doesn't do all the heavy lifting all the time. There has to be balance for it to work. If you both are willing to do whatever it takes and share the workload, you will be just fine. One of my favorite quotes supporting this concept is "No relationship is sunshine all the time, but two people can share one umbrella and survive the storm together." How great is that?

The challenges will come, so don't be afraid. Remember the old saying "What does not kill us will make us stronger." The more prepared you are, the less traumatic and dramatic these times will seem. That is what I am attempting to do here—give you the weapons you need to survive.

There came a time in my marriage when I had to make the choice between my career and the relationship. Even though I enjoyed the salary, travel, and all the accolades that accompanied a career, I wanted the marriage more. Instead of working outside of the home I began helping in the business we own.

I took on the task on paying the bills, preparing the taxes, and putting more energy into taking care of my home. I soon realized something surprising: I enjoyed cooking and cleaning. Who knew? As the days turned into weeks I saw a dramatic change in my husband and our relationship in general.

We began traveling to all the places we'd always wanted to visit. We traveled to Brazil for Carnival, Europe, Mexico, and the Caribbean. Needless to say, the romance between us was at its best. I was not tired from working all day and angry at a demanding boss. My husband changed the way he treated me too. While he had always been good to me, there was a major shift in his overall attitude. He became more loving and generous. He gave me flowers even when there wasn't a special occasion. I found myself cooking more, nothing too fancy, just something home cooked. Now, I am not suggesting that every woman quit her job, but at some point you may have to make some concessions. You may have to decide what's more important—the bigger house, the new car, or quality time with your family. I did not want to become another divorce statistic, so I chose my marriage.

I continued my quest to find the formula, if you will. I came up with what I call the ten tenets of a good marriage. They may not appeal to everyone, but I found them most helpful.

1. Cooking.

Ladies, you don't have to be a five-star chef. Most men will be happy with the most basic meal. If you can cook a meatloaf, open a can of green beans, and add some mashed potatoes you can satisfy the appetites of most men. My grandmother used to say that the way to a man's heart is through his stomach. I agree.

2. Cleaning.

Okay, I know this is a big one. Most men, whether they admit it or not, appreciate a clean home. I hear a lot of women say that their husbands are slobs, and they are tired of cleaning up behind them. I hear you. Let me share something from an article that I read once. A woman wrote to an advice column and asked how to get her husband to clean up after himself. The advice columnist said she should not clean up after him, and let him live in his mess. Of course, I did not agree with that advice.

A reader responded with a story of her own. Her husband was a self-confessed slob. He came home from work and left a trail of clothes throughout the house. She constantly complained, but nothing changed. One day she decided to leave the pile of clothes right where he'd left them. This went on for a few days. At the end of the week, her husband had a massive heart attack and died. She was so distraught that she couldn't bring herself to pick up the clothes and left them on the floor for days. She said she would have given anything to have her husband back so she could pick up after him. She realized what a small thing it was to clean up after a man who worked all day to provide for his family. The moral of the story is, don't sweat the small stuff. Sound familiar?

3. Keep Up Your Appearance

Ladies, we all remember when we were dating our spouses. Most of us—I know I did—went to the salon weekly to have our hair and nails done. We worked out in the gym, managed our weight, and dressed to impress. Why do we discontinue these rituals after we are married? I call this marital amnesia. We forget to do the things that first attracted our husbands to us. After all, we have them now. In addition, we have the kids, the house, the dog, and maybe even a job. Who has time to get to the gym and the salon? I am lucky if I have time to put on some Chapstick.

I hear this all the time. What do you do? You make the time. A little lipstick goes a long way. It doesn't take much to please most men; even the smallest gesture can have an effect. Even if you think he hasn't noticed, trust me—somewhere in his subconscious, he's made a mental note.

Besides, taking care of yourself is as much for you as it is for him.

4. Support Him

"A wise woman knows the importance of speaking life into her man. If you love him: believe in him, encourage him, and be his peace." This quote by Denzel Washington has stayed with me through the years.

The world can be a tough place; when he comes home, be his soft place, his place of peace. Be his biggest supporter, his biggest fan; he will always need his queen. One night, my husband and I were eating at a restaurant with three other couples. I typically order for my husband, because he never wears his glasses when we go out to dinner, and he can't easily see the menu. As usual, I ordered for him. He asked me to pass him the breadbasket. I took out a piece of bread, buttered it, and handed it to him. One of the women at the table said, "I can't believe you order his food and even butter his bread while he waits patiently like a little boy."

She quickly realized what she had said and, from the look on her face, she expected me to be offended. I calmly turned to her and said, "This man works hard to provide for his family. Anything I can do to make him comfortable is my privilege."

One of other women at the table was of Asian descent. She leaned over to me and whispered, "I admire how you look after your husband. In my country, the women look after and take care of their men the way you do."

The husband of the outspoken wife said he wished she took care of him in the same manner. He told my husband how lucky he was to have a woman who made his care a priority. "They don't make woman like that anymore," he said. My husband grinned from ear to ear and agreed that he was a lucky man. I concur. But we ate the rest of our dinner in silence. Not surprisingly, we have not been out to dinner with that couple since then. "A strong woman uses her strength to support her man, not weaken him" is another good quote.

5. Date Him

Remember how much fun it used to be? We'd get all dressed up, waiting for him to pick us up for a date? I spent hours in front of the mirror primping and making sure I looked my best. We held hands and kissed ever so gently and tenderly. Going to the movies and dinner was just the best thing ever.

Again, marital amnesia sets in, and we forget to enjoy each other. Time together doesn't have to be a big production number. It can be something as simple as meeting for coffee and flirting with one another. Every three months, my husband and I spend the night at a local hotel. We pretend we are from out of town, walk around the area, and try and find places we have not been before. We eat at new restaurants. Sometimes we drive an hour out of town and check into a hotel there. The point being, the date doesn't have to be elaborate as long as the two of you focus on each other. As far as you are concerned, work and kids do not exist. Keep the romance alive!

6. Listen to Him

Everyone wants to feel heard, men in particular. Although they deny that they like to talk, they really do. They just want to talk about what is important to them. When your man speaks to you, listen. Truly listen. When he wants to talk, listen without judgment. Be supportive.

My husband likes to work out at the gym. Occasionally, he asks my daughter and me if we can tell he is working out. We stroke his ego and tell him how buff he looks. More often than not, he reaches into his pocket and hands us one hundred dollars. Sometimes we ask if he has been working out just to get the hundred dollars. He knows, of course, what we are doing, but he likes that we listen to him talk about his workouts.

7. Respect Him

Ladies, I know sometimes our husbands can get on our last nerve. Sometimes I need the patience of Job to deal with my husband. By the way, his name is Frank. Even in the most trying of times, we must always show him respect. It gets in my craw when I hear women disrespect their husbands in public. Even if you disagree with him, tap him under the table, if you must, but never call him out in public or in front of others. Every man wants to feel like you are his biggest supporter.

8. Anticipate His Needs

This is a big one. Nothing is more attractive and appealing to a man than a woman who knows what he wants and needs, even before he does. My husband thinks I am psychic. He still can't figure out how I know exactly what he needs 90 percent of the time. Trust me, ladies—men are not that hard to figure out. Most men want three basic things: (1) food, (2) sex, and (3) sports. There are so many little things that you can do to make sure his needs are met.

One thing I do is have his slippers by the garage door when he comes in. His feet are usually cold from working outside all day, so the first thing he looks for are his slippers. If it is really cold outside, I will warm them just before he enters. The look of comfort and relief on his face as his feet slide into the shoes warms my heart.

Occasionally, I spend the day at our business. One day I noticed that his desk and chair showed signs of wear and tear. I went to Office Depot, purchased a new desk and chair, and had it delivered the next day. He called me totally shocked and surprised. He asked how I knew that he wanted a new desk and chair. I just laughed and confirmed his suspicion that I am indeed psychic. If you see that your man could use a new pair of shoes or even some underwear, surprise him. The smallest gestures will mean a lot to him. If you figure out what he needs and furnish it before he asks, you have won the battle, so to speak.

9. Take Care of Him

Ladies, we all know how most men are when it comes to their health. My husband would eat meat and junk food all day if he could get away with it. We must be mindful of their dietary and or medical needs when we prepare their meals.

My husband has a minor issue with his cholesterol, so when I shop for and prepare meals, I keep that in mind. He balked a bit at first when I cut out some of the fatty foods, but I assured him that I did so because I want him around for a very long time.

Make sure he has an annual physical. Most men prefer not to go to the doctor until they are full-on sick. We don't want to wait until that happens. It reminds me of the commercial that showed a wife who stayed attached to her husband's back all day until he agreed to see his doctor. We have to be our partners' health advocate. I schedule Frank's doctor appointments, and I go with him to each visit. I take notes and ask questions. I make darn sure that I know what he needs to do to remain healthy. If your husband takes medication, make sure he adheres to the schedule. As wives, we also take on the role of mother. We care for our children; we must not forget our husbands. In reality, aren't they just little boys anyway?

10. Sports

Okay, ladies, this is a tricky one. If your husband is anything like mine, he is a sports fanatic. His primary passion is *football*. I jokingly refer to myself as a football widow during the season. Sunday, Monday, and now Thursday nights are consumed with football. Now, I must admit in the beginning we had several battles over the amount of time he watched NFL football. The one bright spot was that he didn't watch college sports, or I never would have seen my husband during football season.

After years of back and forth, and me dreading the fall season, I decided to learn more about the sport that dominated so much of my husband's attention. What was so fascinating about men throwing a ball and running up and down a field, not to mention the punishment inflicted on each other. One Sunday I asked Frank to explain the game to me. At first he was a bit annoyed, as he tried to break down what first, second, third, and fourth downs were while trying to watch the game. Then he suggested that we watch the game on Monday night, since the teams playing were, as he put it, lousy. During the course of that game, he explained every play to me. By halftime I had a pretty good understanding of what each team was trying to accomplish. I must admit I still did not get the fascination. I thought to myself, *It must be a man thing*.

Over the years and many Sundays later, as if by magic, I learned to absolutely love the game. Sundays are now my favorite day of the week. I get our football food and beer ready, and we camp out all day and watch the games together when we can. Sometimes we make a friendly wager on the games. It usually involves something intimate.

One Sunday, while we were celebrating our team's victory, Frank kissed me and said, "I really love you." When I asked what had prompted that comment, he said, "I love the fact that we can share something that I enjoy so much." It really meant a lot to him that I respected his love of the game.

After football season has ended, and we are both going through football withdrawal, he takes me on a trip of my choice to thank me for being so understanding. One day he will realize that I love the game as much as he does. Until then, I will continue to enjoy his thank-you gifts.

Ladies, I guess the moral of the story is—if you can't beat them, join them. Remember your husband is at home and not hanging out in a bar all day.

I would like to add a footnote here. Ladies, I know sometimes we wear the S for Superwoman on our chests—working and taking care of the children, home, and spouse—but we must find time for intimacy. We can't allow that crucial part of the relationship dry up. We need that closeness as much as, if not more than, the men in our lives. We need to recharge our batteries, if you will. Make the time.

Finally, never use sex as weapon. I realize that it can be an enticement for getting him to take out the trash or do other tasks around the house, but it should never be used as a weapon. Don't withhold sex or use it as a punishment. Use intimacy to bring you closer, not to separate you. Emotional weapons are never a good idea in relationships. They will only end in disaster.

Marriage Obsolete

"Happy wife, happy life." Who came up with this phrase? I have always thought it was one-sided. It implies that only the wife's happiness matters. As long as she is happy, all is right with the world. Well, that is only half true.

I have found this phrase to be more accurate: "Happy wife, happy life. Happy husband, mate for life." That makes much more sense. Each party's happiness is important. No person's happiness supersedes the other.

"Good relationships don't just happen. They take time, patience, and two people who truly want to be together."

One evening while I was watching TV, I heard a presidential candidate speaking about the recent Supreme Court decision on same-sex marriage. The new ruling requires all states in the union to allow same-sex marriages. The candidate stated that marriage in this country was under attack. He said the secular community wanted to redefine traditional marriage, and he was afraid that marriage as we know it was quickly becoming obsolete.

Marriage becoming obsolete? No way, I thought. *How could such a wonderful institution become obsolete?* I realize that the divorce rate in this country is at an all-time high, and I will discuss that subject in the next chapter, but marriage is not obsolete.

I wondered whether anyone else felt this way. I searched websites and social media for any confirmation of this phenomenon. What I discovered was shocking. According to a recent Pew survey, over 40 percent of Americans feel that marriage is obsolete, compared to only 20 percent in 1978. As I mentioned in an earlier chapter, for the first time in American history, there are currently more single people than married couples.

What is driving this change in attitude toward marriage? What is behind such a dramatic shift in such a short period of time?

One fact I found interesting is that most of the 40 percent who believed marriage to be obsolete were raised either in a single-parent household or by divorced parents (see chapter 4). In addition, most members of this group are millennials—that is, individuals born between 1980 and 2000. As I discussed in chapter 2, with the advent of social media, young people today have more opportunities to meet and hook up. Therefore, the idea of marriage is less appealing, especially if you have no idea what a long-term successful relationship looks like. Studies show that offspring of couples who remain married are more likely to marry and are less likely to divorce than children of divorced parents.

Marriage obsolete? I still was having difficulty absorbing this concept, especially after I just attended a most beautiful wedding. The couple were both in their midthirties. They each grew up in a two-parent household, and both sets of parents had been married more than forty years. It was apparent to all who attended that the young couple was completely in love and looking forward to starting their lives together. Both families joked about wanting grandkids as soon as possible. One mother said she was giving them only one year to present her with a grandchild. You would never have guessed that marriage was obsolete from the love I witnessed at that wedding.

I wanted to delve more into this phenomenon, so I decided to interview three couples. Couple number 1 has been married for five years and has one child. Couple number 2 are newlyweds, married only a few weeks. The third couple, like me, has been married over three decades.

I asked each group a series of questions:

1. What is your current age?
2. Are your parents married or divorced? For how long?
3. How long have you known your partner?

4. Was marriage an easy decision?

5. Do you have or want children?

6. How do you resolve conflicts?

7. How would you describe your marriage?

8. And, finally, would you do all over again? (This is the big question.)

I have to tell you the couples met these questions with serious apprehension. I had to assure each person that I would make the experience as painless as possible, and no couple would be identified by name. After repeated phone calls and free lunches, everyone was on board and agreed to speak candidly with me.

Before I began each interview, I shared one of my favorite quotes:

The couples that are meant to be are the ones who go through everything that's designed to tear them apart but come out even stronger.

This is certainly true for my husband and me, and I hope it is true for the three couples as well.

Couple Number 1

This couple has been married five years and have one child. They both work; he is an accountant, and she is a nurse. He is thirty-five; she is thirty-four. Both sets of parents are living and are still together. The parents serve as examples for the couple and offer guidance, as well as babysitting services.

They met in college when he was twenty-one and she was twenty. They began dating shortly afterward and remained in a relationship for a few years until they wed. They both agreed that during the course of their marriage there have been some difficulties. Spending time together without their child has been their biggest challenge.

They are very fortunate in that they have two sets of grandparents who are always available for babysitting duties. After the birth of the baby, she suffered from postpartum depression, as do a lot of women. She sought advice from her family, as well as from her physician, and for a while used medication until she felt like herself again.

I want to take this opportunity to say that if you feel you need help, please do not hesitate to ask for it. It does not—let me repeat, *it does not*—make you a bad mother. A happy and adjusted mother is a good mother.

When communication problems arise, they both agree to take a breath and a time-out before they engage each other. They don't raise their voices to one another. They are determined to raise their child to understand that while you may not always agree with others, you must always show respect. Wanting to set a good example for their child helps them to maintain control during challenging times.

She is back at work and in her routine and is a happy and adjusted wife and mother. They have biweekly date nights, as well as romantic rendezvous, as often as possible. They seem to have found the balance needed to maintain a successful relationship. There are future plans for second baby, and both agreed that they will continue to make each other a priority. They are determined not to become a divorce statistic. This couple realized very early in the marriage that they needed a village to be successful and were not afraid to lean on others for help and guidance.

Both parties contend that they are happy and "complete"— their word, not mine. Based on what I've seen and heard from these two, I feel optimistic about their future.

Couple Number 2

These newlyweds have been married only a few weeks. Of course, everything is new and bright and shiny at this point. Both are from single-family homes and have not been exposed to many healthy relationships. He is twice divorced; this is her first marriage. He does not have children, but there are challenges that accompany two failed marriages. (For more on this topic, see chapter 4.)

They dated for two years before their marriage. They both work and have equally busy schedules.

One of their major roadblocks has been that she wants children and he does not. I suspect that has to do with his fear of another failed relationship. This was never a serious topic of discussion prior to the marriage. I asked them why they had not discussed such a major issue before. She admitted that she didn't want to scare him off. You can just imagine my next comment: "What were you thinking?"

He'd just assumed that she didn't want children, since she was forty and didn't have any. Remember the statement I made earlier? "Assumption is a relationship killer." Now here they were, both pretty resolute about their positions.

After speaking with them in depth, I feel there is a possibility that, once he becomes more secure in the relationship, he may feel differently. He is not opposed to fatherhood; he just doesn't want his children to become products of a broken relationship one day.

While I understand his concerns, I want him to see that there are no guarantees. Any union might end in divorce. However, if two parties remain committed and do the work, they have protection against the D word.

The couple have agreed to table the subject of children for the time being and concentrate on communicating their desires and needs to one another.

While he has some concerns and trepidations, he feels generally positive about their union. She hears her biological clock ticking, but I believe they need to spend more time communicating and learning more about one another before introducing children into the equation. They both agree. I am hopeful for this couple and will continue to work with them along their journey.

Couple Number 3

The third couple has been married for thirty-one years and has no children. He grew up in the foster care system and never knew his parents. She is from a very loving two-parent home with three siblings. They never had children due to a health issue she had early in their relationship. When I asked if they regretted never having children, in unison, they responded with a resounding no.

His job as an interpreter for the government has taken them all over the globe—Europe, Latin America, and the Far East. Due to his childhood in the foster care system, he finds it difficult to connect to other people. When he met his wife, he found her to be very nurturing and caring. They met at a homeless shelter where they both volunteered. He said it was love at first sight. I'm not sure I believe in that concept, but that's what he said. They dated for six months before getting married in Las Vegas.

They began their travels and adventures around the world. Honesty and openness have been the cornerstones of their relationship from the beginning; as a result, they have had very few conflicts. His lack of a family coupled with her strong family ties and religious upbringing contributed to the enduring commitment they have made to one another.

My final question to them was, as you get older do you think you will regret never having a family? Again in unison, the answer was no. Both stated that with extended family and friends, they don't believe they will ever be alone.

Three vastly different couples from different backgrounds, each finding their way and making their relationships work for them. There is no right or wrong way make it work. You have to find your own formula and decide what works best for the two of you.

Remember this is not your parents' or your friend's relationship. It's yours, and you have to make it work for you. Communication is the key. If you can learn to effectively communicate, you are halfway to having a healthy relationship.

We will talk more extensively about communication in chapter 5.

CHAPTER 4

DIVORCE: WHEN THE RELATIONSHIP FAILS

Divorce is like a death without a burial.

Now that we have talked extensively about relationships and how to survive and thrive in them, let's talk about what happens when you don't. Divorce becomes the final nail in the coffin, which is where your relationship now resides. I recently came across this quote: "The number one reason that marriages that were once good go bad is couples stop putting in the effort." I hear this from couples who are divorced or going through a divorce.

She says, "He stopped paying attention to me, bringing me flowers, and telling me I'm beautiful."

He says, "She stopped making me feel needed, appreciated, and wanted."

Again, they lost the drive to make an effort. Remember what it took to get that person is what it will take to keep them. When you stop putting in the effort, problems will arise.

Let's take a look at some alarming statics surrounding divorce today.

The current divorce rate in the United States is around 50 percent, according to Divorcerate.org. It further states that 60 percent of second marriages and 73 percent of third marriages will end in divorce. These statistics are alarming.

Statistics also show that young women who marry under the age of twenty have a 28 percent divorce rate. That percentage decreases as the number of married years increases. I use this statistic to back up my position when I talk to my daughter about getting married at a young age. Her response is always the same:

"You and dad were married before you were twenty, and here you are still married after thirty-nine years." Then I get the infamous eye roll. It's hard to argue with that; however, we beat the odds using tried and true methods and with help from a village.

Interestingly enough, the United States ranks sixth among the top ten countries with the highest divorce rate, according to Divorcerate.org. The country with the highest rate of divorce is Russia, followed by Belarus, Ukraine, Moldova, Cayman Islands, United States, Bermuda, Cuba, Lithuania, and the Czech Republic. In 2012, Spain, Singapore, Poland and Italy all reported a divorce rate of less than 17 percent. The website also states couples with children have a slightly lower rate of dissolution.

This suggests that couples with children are more willing to work through their issues for the sake of the children. Divorcerate. org also states that 66 percent of all divorce couples are childless. The belief is that the absence of children in a marriage may lead to loneliness and discontent. It makes you appreciate your kids a little more now, doesn't it?

I could add more and more statistics, but you get my point. I wanted to know the underlying causes of such extreme rates of divorce both in the United States and abroad. There is a laundry list of reasons. Let's explore some of the possibilities.

One reason that instantly comes to mind is M-O-N-E-Y.

Several clients tell me that finances played a major role in the dissolution of their marriages. No doubt, the recent financial crisis and housing meltdown were factors influencing the spike in the divorce rate over the course of the last decade.

Early in our marriage, we too experienced money difficulties. We struggled to make ends meet and had to work several jobs just to pay the bills. I'm sure many of you can relate. We were fortunate enough to have family members who were able to assist us.

Money is just one factor, however; several other issues come into play as well. According to a leading Christian website, the top ten reasons for divorce are as follows:

1. Infidelity
2. Lack of communication
3. Physical or mental abuse
4. Financial issues
5. Sexual incompatibility
6. Boredom, lack of excitement
7. Religious and cultural differences
8. Childcare responsibilities
9. Addiction to drugs, alcohol, porn
10. Differences in priorities and expectations

While this list is by no means exhaustive, it does cover the more common reasons for divorce. With so many marriages failing, one might ask, why bother?

We bother because when marriage works, it can be terrific. We do so because we enter marriage believing it will be different for us. We believe our love will beat the odds. Sadly, over half of marriages won't survive. When challenges and difficulties arise, most of us are ill-equipped to handle them. Part of the problem is that there are few role models for marriages today.

Couples often tell me that they thought marriage would be easy—hearts and flowers and sex all day. Most people who have been married for more than five minutes will tell you that is not realistic. My grandmother used to say, "The storms will come; you just have to ride the wave. Eventually the sun will come out, and you will land on the beach with the sun shining down on you." This is my favorite quote, and I use it a lot. I hope you find it as helpful as I have over the years.

Consequences of Divorce

Now, I would like to review the consequences of divorce. The biggest fallout from divorce relates to the children. Studies show that children of divorced parents suffer from lower self-esteem and have greater trust issues. According to a leading Christian website, many of these children have behavioral issues, experience difficulty in school, and suffer from depression.

Promiscuity and addiction are common among these children, and they are at greater risk for divorce themselves. While this is not the case for all children of divorced parents, it holds true for many of them.

Women also suffer from the fallout of divorce. Typically, most women retain physical custody of the children. With the loss of a second income, there is now increased financial pressure on the mother. She now becomes a single parent who faces working and raising the children on her own. A divorced woman has a much more difficult time dating and finding a future mate. Often, her children will blame the new man in her life because Dad is no longer in the picture. And he has to work that much harder to establish his place in the blended family unit. This may put a strain on the new relationship, and Mom will find herself in the awkward position of having to act as referee or appearing to take one side against the other. This can be a very difficult and sensitive position to navigate.

Often children will blame the custodial parent for the demise of the family unit. If you want proof, check out a few episodes of the *Dr. Phil* show. There have been several episodes featuring children angry with their divorced parents. The custodial parent usually bears the brunt of the anger and frustration.

After divorce, many women experience feelings of failure and guilt because they were not able to keep the family together. Self-esteem and sense of self-worth take's a hit among women as well as children. Seventy-five percent of the women I coach are from divorced or single-parent households. Most admit that they did not have positive role models to emulate.

We live in a fast-food society, where everything is disposable and easily replaced. At the first sign of difficulty, off to divorce court we run. When a relationship ends due to a lack of communication or intimacy issues, the individual is more likely to carry these issues into subsequent relationships. Second marriages are sixty times more likely to fail. So you see, divorce is not always the answer or the only option. I am not suggesting that anyone remain in a marriage if there is abuse on any level. But if there is an opportunity to salvage the marriage, especially if children are involved, it's worth the effort.

I recently came across an article by Debra Macleod, a renowned couples mediator and relationship expert. She listed the eight lies that parents on the brink of divorce tell themselves. I could not agree with her more, so I would like to share them with those of you who are currently considering divorce. Ask yourself which one of these apply to you.

1. "My kids want me to be happy." Children want to grow up in a household with both parents who love and respect one another.

2. "My kids will be better off." Children of divorce tend to suffer emotional and behavioral and trust issues at a higher rate and are at greater risk for divorce.

3. "My next relationship will be better." Second and third marriages are at greater risk for divorce than the first.

4. "Nothing will change between myself and my kids." Children tend to blame and resent parents for divorce. In some instances, the children themselves will carry the blame and as well as the shame, believing that they caused the separation.

5. "I won't have any regrets." You probably will look back and wonder at some point if you should have tried harder, especially as you age and have grandchildren and realize that you are no longer the patriarch or matriarch of the family.

6. "We can't stay together for the kids." There is no better reason to stay together than the kids.

7. "Divorce will solve my problems." It won't. You will face a whole new set of problems, worrying about your kids when they are with the other parent as well as the new person in his or her life. Are they being cared for properly?

8. "Kids are resilient." Kids don't adapt; they make do and do their best to cope emotionally.

While divorce may be the only option for a select few, in many cases marriages can be salvaged.

Earlier I listed some of the top reasons for divorce. Infidelity was at the top of the list. While I do believe that infidelity is inexcusable, it does not have to be a deal breaker. Hear me out. Many couples are able to overcome the hurt and anger that occurs after infidelity. Let's look at one couple, very much in the public eye, that was able to work through the public shame and remain married.

Of course, I am describing the Clintons. Hillary was able to move past what was surely a painful time in her marriage and in her life. How was she able to do it? I bet there were many nights when Bill slept on the couch with one eye open. But I'm sure with counseling and time, the trust returned, and the marriage remained intact.

Many people judge her negatively for staying in the marriage. I have no idea why she stayed, but it certainly was her right to do so. Now they are grandparents to a little girl and boy that they can enjoy together.

I understand that for some women infidelity is a deal breaker. And that's okay. Deciding whether to stay or leave is a personal choice. My point is you should not be vilified either way. I just want to show you that you do have a choice.

While divorce may be the only option for some of you, review all your options, and let your conscience guide you. Do not give in to outside or inside pressures.

Anyone considering divorce should seek professional counseling to help you navigate the process. Family counseling can help ease the transition for both you and the children.

> Divorce is like an amputation; you
>
> survive but there is less of you.
>
> —Margaret Atwood

CHAPTER 5

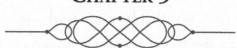

COMMUNICATION: CAN WE TALK?

In a relationship, when communication starts
to fade, everything else will follow.

I love this quote. It hits right at the heart of what happens when two people fail to communicate. Often we think that our spouses should know what we are thinking. We want to believe that the time we've spent together somehow gives them insight to our brains. This is so far from reality. No one is a mind reader.

In the 1970s, there was a magician—the Amazing Kreskin—whose claim to fame was that he could read minds and influence people's thinking. Well, I don't know about you, but I think it would be a bit troublesome if my husband could read my thoughts. If you had the ability, it would be great if you could turn it on and off as required.

Unless you are married to Kreskin, trust me when I tell you that your partner cannot read your mind. There are times when my husband seems to have insight into what I am thinking or feeling, but that is because we have been together for so many years. That being said, we do understand that we can't read each other's minds. You have to open your mouth and speak if you want to be heard and understood. Be open and honest, and tell your partner about your concerns as well as your expectations.

My husband and I have this exercise that we call "checking in." We do this at least once a month. At night, before bed, we check in with each other: Are your needs being met? How can I contribute to your happiness and wellbeing? This must be an open and honest exchange. If there is an area in the relationship that is lacking or needs attention, speak up; now is the time. Don't wait until you're in the middle of an argument to disclose what's missing in the relationship. That admission will be used as a weapon and any conversation about what's lacking will be fruitless. Don't have this conversation during dinner with the children present or as a casual event. Do this intentionally, and take whatever time is needed; don't rush one another. You also don't want to make this a long, drawn-out affair, or it won't be very effective. Try and focus on immediate needs, rather than on the past.

Don't assume that all is well. Remember "assumption is a relationship killer."

If one or both of you identify an area that needs work or attention, put a plan in action. It may be something as simple as having a date night or taking home a bouquet of flowers. If you have children, send them to Grandma's for the weekend so that the two of you can reconnect; this can do wonders for a relationship. The solution doesn't have to be complicated; keep it simple.

One aspect of being a 21st Stepford wife is that you should be a good communicator. Women, remember that men communicate differently than we do. And that's okay. For most men, it's either black or white with very little gray. I don't know about you, but I see things in every shade of the rainbow. This is why communication is so important.

Some of you may remember that popular song by Rupert Holmes, "Escape"; most people called it "The Piña Colada Song."

It was about a man who was bored with his relationship. One night he glanced through the personal ads, and one caught his attention. It had been placed by a woman who was also bored in her relationship. She was looking for someone who liked "piña coladas, getting caught in the rain, making love at midnight, and the taste of champagne." If you are into these things, she said, "come with me and escape." Without much thought, he responded to her ad. His reply was, "Yes, I like piña coladas, getting caught in the rain, making love at midnight, and the taste of champagne." He requested that they meet at a bar called O'Malley's to plan their escape. As soon as she walked in the bar, he recognized her. After a moment, they both laughed and said, "I never knew that you liked piña coladas, getting caught in the rain, making love at midnight, and the taste of champagne." Turns out, they already had what they were looking for all along.

As you can see, the moral of the song is clear: there was a lack of communication in their relationship. Each was ready to run off into the sunset with someone who wanted the same things the other one did. What if someone else had replied to either ads? This is why check-ins are so important. That situation could have been avoided if they'd only had a fifteen-minute conversation.

Even though this was just a song, it must have been reality for someone at some point. I imagine the two of them going home, making love at midnight, drinking champagne, and laughing at the thought of almost losing one another.

Communication Exercise

> Don't assume your partner knows everything you
> expect in a relationship. A relationship should be
> based on communication, not assumptions.

This chapter examines varies ways to communicate. Let me start by saying that there is no one way to communicate, but there is a right way and a wrong way. Yelling and screaming at each other is definitely the wrong way. Pushing each other's buttons and hitting below the belt is ineffective. We've talked about check-ins; now we will look at other effective ways to communicate.

Create a Safe Zone for Communication

Effective communication requires a safe zone where no topic is off limits. Couples need to be able to talk about anything and everything in the safe zone. Whatever is openly discussed in this forum, however, can never be used as a weapon or a bargaining tool at a later date or outside the safe zone. To accomplish this, establish a quiet and safe place. Mine is in a spare bedroom, set up with candles and relaxation music. I wanted a space that is not utilized very often so that it would be seen almost sacred. You don't have to create an elaborate place, just one where you both are comfortable and at ease.

This is not the time to rehash old hurts and open old wounds but to enhance your relationship. Both partners must be open and understanding. No judging is allowed here. In this space we talk about our likes and dislikes, what makes us happy as well as sad. We talked earlier about checking in; describe your needs and what you would like to see happen in the relationship. I was a little apprehensive about all this communication and wondered how my husband would respond to it. As you know, most men don't appreciate talking about their feelings. It's important to make it fun and even a bit sexy. Finger food and a nice bottle of wine will help lighten the mood.

We have an unspoken understanding that the night will end in romance; the better the communication, the better the romance. Stay on course; remained focused. This is not the time to talk about the kids and school or the mortgage. Remember this time is for the two of you to connect or reconnect. I suggest checking in at least once a quarter. You can do this in bed or over lunch. Follow up with your partner to ensure his needs are being met and that there is no discontent brewing under the surface. Again, don't assume.

Do not raise your voice. Speak to each other as if you were in public. You probably would not raise your voice in the doctor's office or in a place of worship. I know this is can be difficult, but in the end you will be glad if you avoid saying something that you really don't mean and can't take back.

Remember—just because you're mad at your partner doesn't mean you don't love him. Another favorite quote of mine is "Most relationships fail because we spend too much time pointing out each other's mistakes and not enough time enjoying each other's company."

Remember "relationships are not only about holding hands when you understand each other and are in agreement; [they are] about having lots of misunderstandings and still holding each other's hand[s]."

Use the "Did You Know ..." Tool

Start by asking the other person, "Did you know _____?" Fill in the blank with something about yourself that he may not know. For instance, I asked Frank, "Did you know that I want to go to Comic Con dressed as Wonder Woman?" He looked a bit surprised at first and then burst out laughing. He said, "I never knew that" and suggested that I not tell anyone else. He followed up with "Did you know I wanted to be a race car driver?" I never knew that.

You can throw in something like "Did you know I hate carrots?" or "Did you know I like it when you kiss my neck?" It can virtually be anything that comes to mind. There are no limitations. Have fun and be creative. The object is to share information about yourself that your partner may not know.

My husband and I do this exercise from time to time. You will be surprised the things you can learn. Sometimes, the lessons are extremely funny; at other times, they are eye opening. It's a simple way to continually learn about your partner.

Above all, you must keep the lines of communication open, even at times when it may be difficult. Communication is as vital to a relationship as water is to our bodies. Without water, we would dehydrate, and our bodies would die. Without effective communication, our relationships will wither and die.

Take a few minutes and think about the ways you can enhance your communication skills. Use the next page to take notes and keep track of your progress. List the skills you have learned during the course of your relationship. What worked, and what didn't work?

Try some of the techniques I've listed. Did they change the way you communicate? How? What could you have done differently? What worked best for you? Use the next page to document your activity. It helps to be able to refer back to a visual guide.

CHAPTER 6

CAN WE REALLY HAVE IT ALL?

This is the age-old million-dollar question: Can women really have it all? We've talked about dating, marriage, and divorce, but I wonder if it is realistic to think that women can have marriage, family, and career simultaneously.

Women today wait until much later in life to marry. They put more energy into their careers and personal development. Women also are having children much later in life than they did twenty-five years ago. As stated in chapter 3, for the first time, there are more single people in the United States than at any other time in history. Men are even waiting a longer period of time before they pop the question. In most major metropolitan cities, women outnumber men—in some cases by 2:1 or even 3:1. Many women tell me that developing a successful career is much easier than finding a husband.

Finding a husband can be like the proverbial needle in a haystack. I watched a movie in which Julia Roberts played a graduate student who taught history at a women's college during the 1950s. She found that most of the young ladies were seeking a degree in an effort to find a husband and had no intention of having a career after graduation. The degree was intended to make them more appealing to "the right man." They were less concerned about obtaining a BA and more focused on becoming a Mrs.

That was typical of that era; the goal was to get married, have children, and keep house. Of course, there is nothing wrong with that, if it is your choice.

The 1960s rolled in with a bang, and women decided overwhelmingly that they wanted more. Women now were afforded a variety of opportunities; marriage was no longer their only option. We enjoyed our newfound freedom, and so did men.

The explosion of the sexual revolution eliminated the need to wait until marriage to have sex. As a result, men no longer felt the pressure to marry, certainly not as quickly as they had in the past.

Women's views on marriage and relationships began to shift. We were told and believed that we could have it all. We no longer had to choose between marriage, family, and a career. "I am woman; hear me roar" became a New Age mantra. Remember that catchy tune by Helen Ready?

I am woman; hear me roar. If I have to, I can do anything. I am strong. I am invincible. I am woman. You can bend but never break me; I will come back even stronger.

Well, you know the rest. The song certainly sounded great at the time and was greatly needed. I do think, however, it gave women a false sense about how much we can really accomplish simultaneously.

Yes, we are strong. We give birth and, minus the screaming, we make it look easy. (Incidentally, yes, ladies, you do deserve a push present.) But at some point we have to accept that we can't do and have it all. I'm sorry, but it's the truth. Most of you already know this.

Can we really have it all? There have been many stories in the news lately about women and men leaving their babies in hot cars, resulting in injury and even death. Each time the parent stated that he or she was in a hurry, became distracted, and forgot the baby was in the back of the car.

In 2017 alone, at least twenty infants and young children died from auto-related heat stroke. Since 1998, almost seven hundred confirmed deaths have been reported. I bet the number is much greater. Even one is a sheer tragedy. Our schedules have become so hectic and hurried that it they are impossible to juggle. Again, I wondered, where did the concept of having and doing it all originate? Was it only from the "I Am Woman" song? How and when did this concept come into being?

I did a little bit of research. It seems to have taken shape in the early 1960s during the women's rights movement. Some of you may remember women burning their bras in the street and declaring their liberation. Women were protesting for equal rights and equal pay. We made great strides but with some unintended consequences.

The editor-in-chief of a popular magazine informed women of the 1960s that we could have it all. She told her readers that we could have successful careers, marriages, and families all rolled up in a neat little package. She held up her life as the example. She had all these things and was happy as well. Truth be told, she was a woman of means with a housekeeper, assistant, and many others in her life to help navigate her days. Now wouldn't it be great if we all had housekeepers, nannies, and assistants to help with our daily tasks? Most women can only dream of this type of life. Because we achieved some of the rights we fought for, we were conditioned to believe that we were Wonder Women and could do and have it all.

Advertisers quickly jumped on the band wagon and designed commercials around this concept. Remember the cigarette ad that told us, "You've come a long way, baby"? Or that the Enjoli perfume commercial in the 1980s, the one where the woman sings, "I can bring home the bacon, fry it up in a pan, and never let you forget you're a man." The commercial implied that a woman could do all these things and never break a sweat.

The actress in the commercial made it look so easy, didn't she? Well, we know that it's not that easy. Work eight hours or more a day, raise a family, take care of the household and a dog, and maintain a personal relationship; it makes me exhausted just to write it. Is it realistic to think that we can juggle all these balls in the air and not drop one from time to time? As women we all have to don Wonder Woman capes from time to time, but how long can we keep up the facade? For some of you, the answer may be "as long as it takes." Is it realistic to think that we can work forty or more hours a week, ferry the kids to basketball practice or dance recitals, help with homework, cook dinner, do laundry, and tend to our spouses? My goodness, we do have Wonder Woman's cape under our clothes. If only we had her golden lasso to help with our tasks.

What we do is get through our days the best way we know how. For most of you that means plenty of coffee and very little sleep. So my question remains: Can we really have it all—the successful career, well-adjusted children, and a happy spouse?

I was watching TV one night, an old movie from the 1980s I had not seen in a while. Called *Baby Boom*, it starred Diane Keaton. The movie centered around a successful female advertising executive. She was in a relationship with a man who did not want to have children. This wasn't a problem as she felt the same way. She loved her job, and her superiors loved her killer business instinct. All was right within her world until one day the unthinkable happened.

She receives a phone call from the lawyer of a distant relative who had passed away and left her something in her will. She meets the lawyer at the airport to get this inheritance and is handed a baby girl. Shocked, she asks, "What am I supposed to do with the baby of a cousin I have not seen in years?" Well, she takes the baby home and begins calling adoption agencies.

But while she's waiting to find a suitable parent for the baby, she falls in love with the adorable child. To everyone's amazement, she decides to keep the baby, Elizabeth. What she does not anticipate is the resistance she encounters from the man in her life and her employer. Let's just say, they are not amused. The boyfriend leaves, and the employer fires her. I'm sure some of you have had similar experiences.

She decides to buy a farm and raise the baby alone. All goes well; she meets a nice guy and starts a small baby food company using the produce she grows on the farm. Her former employer finds out about the baby food product and makes her a very lucrative offer for her company, including an offer of employment. The offer is so tempting that she considers it for a brief moment. In the end, she walks away from the money and the job offer. She likes her new life. She and Elizabeth are happy living on the farm, and she likes being able to stay home and raise her daughter. Even this fictional character realizes that she cannot have it all. I'm sure some of have come to the same realization.

Another movie exemplifying this point is *The Devil Wears Prada*. The movie centers on a very successful magazine editor. While she may be the best in the business, her third husband has filed for divorce, and her twins were raised by their boarding school. Her intern initially finds the lifestyle frivolous but grows to enjoy the perks. Soon her relationship and her friendships begin to suffer. She realizes the job and perks are not worth what she's had to give up. She does not want to go through marriages and relationships like she goes through new shoes. Ultimately, she walks away from it all. This is another fictional character, but I can't help believe that there are similar stories out there somewhere.

I read an article about Indra K. Nooyi, the CEO of PepsiCo, in the *Huffington Post*. She was interviewed by David Bradley, former owner of the *Atlantic*, who asked her to share her success story. She explained that her mother was completely unimpressed with her new position. She talked about the long days and nights she spent at the office, often missing events at her children's school. One late evening, she was informed that she had been promoted to the position of CEO. Well, obviously she was excited and proud and couldn't wait to go home and share the good news with her family. When Nooyi got home, before she could say anything, her mother told her to go to the store and get milk. She got the milk, returned home, and excitedly shared the news of her promotion.

Her mother said, "You might be the CEO and you may be on the board of directors of a major corporation. But in this house you are the wife, the daughter, the daughter-in-law, and the mother." She told her daughter to leave her dammed crown in the garage. She was totally unimpressed with the news.

She sounds a lot like my grandmother.

Nooyi was asked whether women could have it all. He response was candid and honest. She replied, "I don't think women can have it all. We pretend we have it all." She stated that if her daughters were asked if she were a good mom, she was not sure what they would say. I respect her honesty. She was extremely brave to tell her story as she did.

Shonda Rhimes, the creator of the three most popular shows on TV, admitted in an interview that women can't have it all, at least not at the same time. If you are successful in one area, another area suffers.

Two of the most powerful and influential women in the workplace today acknowledge and accept the fact that is difficult and challenging to maintain a successful career, marriage, and family simultaneously. Keep in mind, these are financially secure women who can hire nannies and live-in help, and even they find it difficult to juggle all the balls in the air.

So we are back to the age-old question: Can a woman have a successful career, be a present mother, and be a good wife at the same time?

My opinion is yes, to a degree; however, it takes a village of people surrounding you to make that happen. There will be missed recitals and basketball games. You will feel like you are a circus act, juggling several balls at one time. Sometimes you will drop a ball or two, but don't beat yourself up. Remember you are only human.

Even though my preference is home and family first, I realize that it is not an option for every woman. To those of you who have no choice or have chosen to have careers, I say, get your team in place to help you keep those balls in the air, and set attainable priorities for yourself and your family.

And by all means, never be afraid to ask for help. Don't wait until you pass out on the soccer field from exhaustion or experience symptoms of a heart attack before you accept you are not Wonder Woman. Below are a few golden rules for balancing those balls. They will help keep you on track:

- Get your team members in place—family, neighbors, friends, and so on.
- Set priorities; you can't be in five places at one time.
- Don't be afraid to ask for help.
- Never forget to take care of yourself; you can't take care of others if you don't take care of yourself.
- Limiting the number of activities in which your children are involved doesn't make you a bad mother. Remember there is only one of you.
- Give yourself a break. I'm sure you are doing the best you can.
- Don't be afraid to say no; get over that need to please everyone.

Feel free to add to this list; these are just a few basics.

I recently had an eye-opening experience. I agreed to babysit a four-year-old for five days while his mother was in the hospital. Mind you, I have not spent an extended amount of time with a small child in quite some time. As I have shared with you, I have one adult child. This four-year-old was a very smart and inquisitive little boy. After five days—getting him ready for school, picking him up in the early afternoon, entertaining him, feeding him, and getting him ready for bed—I must admit that I was truly exhausted. And I didn't have to work a full-time job.

I have so much respect for you mothers and women who do this work, day in and day out. It is truly a labor of love. My babysitting experience convinced me even more that it takes a village to get the job done. It reminds me of the scene in the *Sex and the City* movie, when the character named Charlotte thought her husband was having an affair with the nanny. She was more upset about losing the nanny than she was about her husband. Her character received a lot of criticism from moms who didn't have nannies. I respected the fact that she expressed an honest emotion and concern. She realized that she needed help and was honest enough to admit it. That takes courage and does not deserve criticism. If you can manage without help, that's great, but ladies, we need to support one another and not judge those who admit that they need help.

Don't be shy about asking for help. It doesn't mean you're weak, it only means you're wise.

—ILiketoQuote.com

CHAPTER 7

A HUSBAND'S WORDS OF WISDOM

T his book is primarily about women and how they can have happy and healthy relationships, but I want to offer a male perspective. You've heard a lot from my wife about me and our relationship. She shared intimate details about our trials and tribulations and how we overcame them. Although I may be a bit biased, I can tell you that I am one very lucky man to have such a woman in my life.

I'd like you to see her through my eyes. Obviously, I think she is beautiful, as well as intelligent. I could not ask for a better partner in life. I know she talks a lot about pleasing a man, but don't think for one second that it is one-sided; it is not only appreciated but reciprocated. The way she takes care of me, as well as the things she does for me, is greatly appreciated and makes me the envy of my male friends.

Through her behavior, she's taught me how to treat a woman. I enjoy seeing the smile on her face when I bring flowers home in the middle of the week, although no special occasion is at hand. I have the utmost respect for her when we are in public and she goes out of her way to make sure there is no shellfish in my food—I have a food allergy to shellfish. She will even taste test the food to make sure it's safe for me to eat. She doesn't care who is watching. I have watched her time and time again make sure that I don't ingest anything to which I may react while taking a ribbing from some of the guests about it. She politely smiles and announces that it is her job and privilege to take care of me. I know this may sound old-fashioned or out of touch by today's standards, but it's one of the many reasons I love her so much.

As she's shared with you, we own our business. I am always

asked why I work so hard and why I don't take off from work more often. My answer is always the same: I work hard so that my wife and daughter don't have to. I want them to have all the luxuries and comforts that I can afford to give them. There is absolutely nothing I would not give to or do for my wife. So, you see, while she does take care of me, I try my best to back give as much, if not more.

I would like to say to all the men who may be reading this—and I hope there will be some—take care of your woman and make her feel loved and special, and I guarantee she will do the same for you. Tell her often how much you appreciate all that she does for you and the family. Men, let me tell you: if you want some special attention, if you know what I mean, nothing will make that happen faster than offering to do the dishes. If you see that she is tired, get the kids ready for bed so that she can take a long bath. Do the laundry; even something as small as taking out the trash can have a tremendous impact.

Women do not want to feel that the entire responsibility of the family falls squarely on their shoulders. Remember, as my wife often reminds me, a relationship is a partnership.

Trust me—nothing will make you sexier to your partner than doing the dishes. I can't boil water, but if you can put something edible together a few nights a month, it will endear you to your spouse. And, fellows, remember most women love flowers and a nice card, particularly when there isn't a special occasion.

It's not rocket science; just let her know that she is appreciated, and lend a hand from time to time. If you do this, watching football on Sunday will be much more enjoyable. And, by the way, I do know that my wife enjoys football as much as I do. I let her think that it is all me, but who cares? In the end we have a healthy and happy relationship, and isn't that what really matters?

CONCLUSION

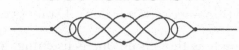

Writing this book has been a true labor of love. I wanted to share with readers what I have learned and still learn every day about marriage and relationships. I challenge you to continue to learn about your partner. I guarantee that as much as you think you know, there is always more to learn. I can watch the same movie several times and always seem to see something I had not noticed before.

I've watched *The Notebook* five times, and each time I experience something new. This is a movie I recommend all couples watch together. Ladies, it may take a little coaxing on your part to get him to watch a chick flick—I know. But it will be worth it to see two people share love that spans several decades; in the end, they can't imagine living without each other. Well, that's the stuff of dreams. My husband tells me all the time not to leave before he does, as if I can control that. I tell him I will do my best.

I am reminded of the poem with the line "may I live as long as you minus one day so that I never have to know a day without you." I hope all of you reading this book have many years of shared happiness. The final piece of advice I want to impart is this: always remember to have fun together, and never stop laughing. Dance; nothing brings two people closer than dancing together. You don't have to have rhythm—we certainly don't. Dance as though no one is watching. Laugh as though no one is listening. Share joy that only you two can feel. Fall in love over and over again.

I hope this book will help you have a happy and healthy relationship.

Best wishes.

ABOUT THE AUTHOR

Married 39 years. Background in Communication.

Certified Life Coach for 5 years working with couples and women who have difficulty achieving personal and relationship success. One child (daughter) who is a social media relations director.

Currently resides in Atlanta Georgia.

Years of working with couples facing relationship difficulties and being asked repeatedly how I make marriage not only work but make it look good lead me to write this book. I wanted to share with other like minded women what I have learned over the last 39 years. Marriage does not have to be scary or a mystery, it just takes a little guidance and help.

I was fortunate enough to have women who guided me and bestowed wisdom which enabled me to navigate the complexities of marriage. My desire is to pay it forward to other women.

My goal is to save as many couples as I can from the devastating grip of Divorce.

Stepfordwife21century@outlook.com

@21cstepfordwife (twitter)

21st Century Stepford Wife (Facebook)

21stcenturystepfordwife.com

21stcenturystepfordwife (instagram)